FALL MAGIC
JOSEPH VON EICHENDORFF

TRANSLATED BY
EDWARD FORD

"Fall Magic," translated by Edward Ford. ISBN 978-1-60264-367-3.

Published 2009 by Virtualbookworm.com Publishing Inc., P.O. Box 9949, College Station, TX 77842, US. ©2009, Edward Ford. All rights reserved. No part of this publication may be reproduced, stored in a retrieval system, or transmitted in any form or by any means, electronic, mechanical, recording or otherwise, without the prior written permission of Edward Ford.

Manufactured in the United States of America.

FOR REVEREND CHESTER VICTOR FORD

BY THE SAME AUTHOR

Alain-Fournier and *Le grand Meaulnes* (*The Wanderer*)

Jean Giono's Hidden Reality

Close Readings of the Work of American Poet Delmore Schwartz (1913-1966)

Rereading F. Scott Fitzgerald: the authors who shaped his style

The Oriental Poems of Leconte de Lisle by Charles-René-Marie Leconte de Lisle (Translation)

The Solitude of Compassion by Jean Giono (Translation)

The Vicar's Passion by Honoré de Balzac (Translation)

TABLE OF CONTENTS

PREFACE

I n this work, Edward Ford has undertaken to translate into English many of the poems and one tale by the nineteenth-century German writer Josef Freiherr von Eichendorff. His achievement is to have brought to readers' attention the beauties of important poetry not widely known in the United States at the present time. Many of these poems have been set to music by composers as distinguished as Schumann, Mendelssohn, Brahms, and Richard Strauss. The musical setting of Eichendorff's poem *In einem kühlen Grunde* by an obscure Lutheran pastor, Friedrich Glück, has become so familiar to present-day Germans that it is often mistakenly listed as a "folk song" in catalogues. Eichendorff's poems are culturally so central to the German lyric tradition that they deserve to be better known in English.

Edward Ford translates *In einem kühlen Grunde* under the title "The Broken Ring." As he notes in his introduction, he has not sought to reproduce the meter and rhyme of the originals. This choice frees him to concentrate on the spirit of the poetry. While translations that follow the rhyme and meter are certainly useful to singers and musicians, they often force translators to use highly stilted and artificial language in English that runs counter to the poems' deeply felt content. It is Ford's merit to have given readers a rendering of this poem and many others in unaffected and natural English that conveys much of the power of the German original to speak directly to the emotions.

Eichendorff wrote about themes at heart of German romantic poetry: about forests, rivers, bird song, sunshine, the seasons, and a rural landscape dominated by castles, water mills and farms. He wrote about *Wanderlust*, the urge to roam and the pleasures of a peripatetic life, such as could be enjoyed by university students and journeymen apprentices. These subjects were "romantic" because in

I

Eichendorff's era there was already a sense that this world was threatened, was coming to an end. In the poet's formative years, Napoleon's armies passed through Germany twice, once on the march eastward, and then in retreat from the failed campaign in Russia. For a number of years in Eichendorff's youth, Prussia was occupied by French forces. By the mid-1820s, railways and industry were beginning to transform the German landscape. Industrialization and war could threaten--and sometimes devastate-- the German landscape, but German poets could both recall and imagine a free space that was peaceful and pristine.

These poems represent more than mere escapism, however. They express a profound love of nature felt at the time--and now-- by many Germans, a deep sense of appreciation for and connection to the land around them, an awareness of the beauties of nature. As Ford points out, these themes possessed an affinity for Americans of the "hippie" generation, but not only for them. As ecological concerns move to the foreground in Americans' awareness, Eichendorff's poetry continues to speak to us, and the translations of these works are most welcome in 2007, the 150th anniversary of the poet's death.

Deborah Schneider, Ph.D.
Lecturer in German
Harvard Divinity School

ACKNOWLEDGMENTS

Thanks to Dr. Deborah Schneider, Dr. Lyman Leathers, Dr. Lewis Overaker, Rev. Victor Ford, Pat Kozma, the Edwin Mellen Press, and my friends everywhere.

INTRODUCTION

F reiherr Joseph von Eichendorff, in both his poetry and his
prose, was a modern minnesinger who sang of all that was
manly, beautiful, and healthy in this life. He sang of rampant
wanderlust, the stunning beauty of the mountains and forests, and of
love for idealized women in castles who would lean out their
windows and listen to his songs. Preeminently musical, he was a
modern minstrel who would follow his whims to Italy where the
lemon groves grow, and then return tired but exalted to his forest
castle in Germany. Eichendorff was ever-restless, yet also a
religious Romantic who longed for the seemingly carefree life of
the Middle Ages. One scholar, Alexander von Bormann, has aptly
stat ed that "Eichendorff was thoroughly prejudiced again st the
Moderns" (Michael Kessler and Helmut Koopmann. *Eichendorffs
Modernität* [Tübingen: Stauffenburg, 1989], 9). He longed to go
back in time historically --he has been called "the last Romantic
knight" (Kessler 58)--but also personally, as throughout his life he
"remained oriented toward his childhood and early youth" (Egon
Schwarz, *Joseph von Eichendorff*, [New York: Twayne, 1972], 14).
His nostalgic songs are well known, since they have been set to
music many times, and many of the best of them are included here.
Eichendorff's energetic novella *The Life of a Good-For-Nothing* has
become famous the world over through translations into all major
languages. Now, with the publication of this volume, we gain a
greater appreciation of his poetry that, which in America has not
been previously translated. Now we can enjoy a gripping story
about mental illness--specifically seasonal affective disorder.

Perhaps it will help our understanding of Eichendorff's work to
recall that in the mid-1950s the Beat movement in literature
developed and was soon followed by the hippies of the 1960s.
These artistically-minded young people liked to wander about

1

reciting poetry and singing songs, and although they could at times become negative about the Vietnam War, at bottom, the movements were about an unbounded love for nature, humanity, and self-expression. Eichendorff, as he reveals himself in his literary oeuvre, would have fit right in with the Beats, and it is surprising that his work was not adopted by the youth of America at that time. Perhaps this was because his work was simply too positive to be considered relevant in the nuclear age.

Yet, his work is relevant. Now, more than ever, in our angst-ridden century, we need poets to redirect us toward the beauties of life, to the beauties of nature, and to the beauties of art. The poetry and prose of Joseph von Eichendorff teach us what it means to be fully alive in the present moment, here, now, today, in an age when a magical moment is just around the corner of the eye.

Freiherr Joseph Karl Benedikt von Eichendorff was born in Upper Silesia--a part of Austria that had recently been taken by Prussia in the Seven Years War and which is now part of Poland--in the Lubowitz Castle, on March 10, 1788. He attended school in Breslau and Halle. In 1807, he began studying at Heidelberg and, in 1810, moved on to Vienna. In 1813, he fought for liberty from the Napoleonic yoke. In 1815, he married Aloysia von Larisch and published his first novel *Presentiment and the Present Age*. The novel was poorly received and languished in obscurity until recently rescued by modern critics for whom "it has assumed the role of a major work" (Robert O. Goebel, *Eichendorff's Scholarly Reception: a survey* [Columbia, SC: Camden House, 1993], 14). Throughout the novel, the prose passages are interspersed with poetic gems, and the prose itself is quite poetically charged with connotative resonances. It is in this wonderfully adventurous novel that Eichendorff wrote his famous line--"the poet is the heart of the world" (Kessler 10)--and he sought to be this heart, to speak for all humanity of love and music and mountains and forests. In short, he loved life, and he communicated this love in his vibrant songs.

In 1816 Eichendorff began his career as a civil servant, and Eichendorff scholar Egon Schwarz has mused:

His performance as a punctilious government official, faithful

2

husband, and loving father does not seem to have any connection with the carefree, unattached characters of his fiction whose perpetual migrations their sedentary creator never ceased to extol as a moral virtue (Schwarz 13).

Yet he had done enough wandering in his youth to fill his imagination for the rest of his life with images of carefree fiddlers sleeping in the forests and delighting village crowds.

In 1821 he was named as a Catholic councillor to the Royal Government at Danzig, and unfortunately in the following years, he saw the final loss of all claims to his childhood castle in Silesia. In 1824 he was transferred to Königsberg. The year 1826 saw the completion of his masterwork *The Life of a Good-For-Nothing*. In 1831 he moved to Berlin where he worked for the Ministry of Education, and all of this time he was writing stories and poems. His second novel, *Poets And Their Friends*, was published in 1834. In 1837 his collected poems were published, and he retired in 1844 to begin translating Spanish dramas. In 1855 his wife died, and the great poet himself died in 1857, thus ending one of the noblest, purest, most heartfelt literary careers that has ever blessed the pages of world literature.

The particularly exciting element in all of Eichendorff's work is "the powerful lyrical component that permeates every aspect of his oeuvre" (Goebel 2); but we are also impressed by the fact that his work is suffused with "a romantic religiosity" (Kessler 121). In these powerfully pungent poems and story, the natural world is always seeping into the minds of the characters, and there is a constant eruption of the past into the present (Goebel 6). The past comes alive; it has never vanished, but lives on in the mountain ruins and the living hearts of the people. According to Egon Schwarz, "there exist undeniable tensions between Eichendorff's conception of poetry and his religious faith. What is more, these tensions lend his creative work a vibrating energy, without which it would be lacking an important dimension" (Schwarz 15). This ever-present tension is a good thing, for it shows Eichendorff's characters stretched between earthly and heavenly longings, regaling themselves in the beauties of nature, but longing for the divine companionship that will only be found in death. This ultimately religious tension is present in the current volume, as Eichendorff seeks to bond with the natural world, even as he desires to transcend it, for his "characters are torn between earthly and heavenly love" (Schwarz 16). Also, according to Schwarz, "His is a pantheistic thought" (Schwarz 15) that blends pagan deities and fidelities with his devout Catholicism. Along these lines, Eichendorff once wrote that "A song sleeps in all things" (Schwarz 15); and this is indeed what he seeks to express: the hidden harmonies, the secret music that underlies all life on this planet, the vital elan that is both in and beyond all things.

In a typically dramatic mood, Eichendorff once wrote, "If in the forest the fairy's glance strikes you and does not burn you to ashes. Then move on, you will never be a poet!" (Schwarz 17). He himself was continually burnt to ashes, and his verses are branded onto our hearts with the molten metal of their precise rhyme schemes--schemes that I have not sought to reproduce in this current volume. In this collection, we find stellar favorites such as "Longing," "The Happy Wanderer," and "The Wandering Musician," for a veritable feast of poetic musicality. Eichendorff's poems sing their way off the pages and into our hearts with their innate lyricism and melodic diction, while his characters and situations are pleasing to our beauty-craving minds.

After feasting on these festive poems, I offer you a chaser in the form of Eichendorff's vivid tale "Fall Magic," though I feel that I must warn you that the magic of the title is a black magic or, more specifically, mental illness. This tale is particularly relevant to me, because I, too, have suffered from seasonal affective disorder, and just like Raymond in the story, my illness, brought on by the blackness of the Norwegian winter night, involved auditory hallucinations and lasted for years before casting me ashore like a dazed Robinson Crusoe wondering where I was at last. Seasonal affective disorder generally starts in the fall and lasts all winter long as the shorter daylight causes one to become depressed and lethargic, and often it is counterbalanced by a great sense of energy in the summer months when there is more sunlight. For centuries, Northern Europeans have been travelling south in the winter to escape the darkness, and writers such as Ibsen often chronicle people whose lives have been blighted by the darkness, and even blackness of a winter without sunlight. One rather well-known example of this is Spanish writer Leopoldo Alas's story about the year spent on the Island of Spitzbergen, in which the character suffers from madness.

This particular tale is structured by the character's relationship to the sun. Near the outset, the character, Raymond, states, "The fall sun remained lovingly warm over the colorful clouds, which decorated the valleys around my castle." Later, we are told "The setting sun cast its rays right across this lovely height, on the wells and the windows of the castle, interspersed with flashes." And as his madness deepens, "It grew dark. Then an earnest nobility spread over her entire body." Later we are told of the ominous darkness:

So I met the night extending through the forest. The entire heavens had changed, and it had become dark, a wild storm raged over the mountains. "We will never see each other again, unless he dies!" I called out loudly within myself and ran as if I were being hunted by ghosts.

And then later, toward the end of the tale, when Raymond realizes that he has been living a hallucination, we read:

Disoriented Raymond turned his face from the frightful silent image and looked at the bright day before him. Then suddenly the beautiful magic woman came up from below on a thin horse, laughing, in full bloom of youth, and passed by. Silver summer clothes flew behind her, the aster from her star cast long green and gold shimmerings over the heath.

This darkling tale, which contains dreams within dreams, as Raymond gets lost in a world of harrowing hallucinations, will touch the heart of anyone who has ever known anyone with mental illness. The prose positively sparkles with all of the vibrant life that we have come to expect from High Romanticism.

Eichendorff's tale probably derives from legends surrounding the great Emperor Frederick Barberossa, though the direct source, as in "Rip Van Winkle," is the legend of "Peter Klaus." According to Eichendorff scholar Friedrich Weschta, this tale "must be

considered an early version of the novella ['The Marble Statue']"
(Goebel 29), yet it is so different from the later story--which has
already appeared in English--that it stands alone and charms us all
on its own. Weschta has shown that the story probably derives from
Tieck's *Der Getreue Eckbert und der Tannhäuser* (Goebel 29), but
was also influenced by "*Der Runenberg* (1824), *Der Blonde
Eckbert, Die Freunde* (1797), and other stories such as *Die Elfen*
(1812) provide various motifs" (Goebel 29). Yet there is another
source that is very significant, and that is Ovid. Eichendorff was
familiar with Ovid's *Metamorphoses* (Kessler 204); and the way the
themes and characters change shape in the story is certainly
derivative of the great Latin author. In particular, there is a notable
scene of the bathing beauties at the center of the story:

A still fish pond lay in the circle of the high cliffs, which
extended their ivy and their ledge flowers. Many women bathed
their beautiful limbs while singing in the waving waters up and
down. Above them all stood a woman splendid and without clothes
and looking on, while the others sang and fell silent in the
harmonious play, swishing their fingers in the waters as if charmed
and bathing in the image of their own beauty, so that the drunken
mirror of the water glistened.

This scene would seem to be a direct reference to Ovid's
famous scene of Diana in her bath, which is a scene that appears in
the Bible as the legend of David and Bathsheba, and which
significantly is contained in a fuller version in the Korean folktale,
"Sonya wa Namukun," or "The Fairy and the Woodcutter." The
Korean version of the tale not only has a supernatural dimension,
but is clearly an astrological myth; for, after watching the fairies
bathe, the Woodcutter is raised up to the stars in a Big Dipper. What
is fascinating about this Korean connection, in addition to the
hunters and the bathing beauties in both stories, is that Eichendorff's
hero, in being affected by the loss of light in the fall season, is also
being affected by the heavenly stars. This relating of humans to the
stars is what the "re-linking" of "religion" was originally all about,
and it is found in the Korean version, too.

Thus, in this single volume, we have a fitting tribute to a

German master of poetry, prose, scholarship, and translation, who deserves to be celebrated once again as we approach the 150th anniversary of his passing, in 2007. Eichendorff's work belongs to the first wave of Romanticism. These poems and this story helped herald a thoroughly new Romantic voice in literature--one that has gone on to resound throughout the centuries and which still speaks to us today. Let us enjoy them anew or for the first time in this modern translation, and may Eichendorff's precious poems and prose last for as long as humanity has a need to seek succor in the dappled pages of foliate books.

(Edward Ford, Lexington, Massachusetts, 2007)

The Wanderer's Songs

Refreshing Travel

Fresh winds come flowing blue
Spring, spring so it must be!
Bugle calls pierce the forest,
As moody eyes shine with light;
The confusion has color, ever more color,
Becomes a magical, wild river,
In the beautiful forest down below
Enticed by the river's greeting.

And I don't want to worry!
When the wind drives me far from you,
I will travel on the river,
Blinded by the delightful gleam!
Thousands of enticing voices shout,
High Aurora whirls in flames,
Go now! I don't want to know
Where the trip will take me!

General Wandering

From the forest floor up to the peaks
As far as eye can see,
All the tree-tops are greening,
So let us go a-wandering:

Springs from the cliffs,
Rivers on the plains,
Larks high in air;
A happy poet standing before them.

Those in the valley age

Trapped in gloomy cares
He wants to recruit them all
For wonder-filled wandering.

And all down the mountains
He shouts his song into the valley
Where his scattered brethren
Suddenly feel homesick.

Then the whole world becomes cheerful
And takes up its travelling shoes,
While his girl down below
Signals secretly to him.

And over the cliff walls
And upon the green expanse
Everything blends, and rejoices ceaselessly
So let us go a-wandering!

THE HAPPY WANDERER

The one whom God truly favors
He sends out into the wide, wide world;
And shows His mighty wonders
In mountain, forest, stream, and field.

The dullards sleeping at home,
Are not refreshed by dawn's pure red,
All they know from cradle on
Are sorrows, burdens, and want of bread.

Springs stream from the mountains,
Larks fly as high as they wish,
Why shouldn't I sing along with them
With full throat and fuller breast?

I just let our loving God govern;
All the brooks, larks, forests, and fields;
And heaven and earth will show,
That he also arranges things best for me.

THE BROKEN RING

A mill-wheel turns
In a cool valley
My true love is gone
Who once lived there.

She gave me her word,
And a ring along with it,
She broke her word,
And my ring broke in two.

I want to wander
Like a minstrel through the world
Singing all my sorrows
And going from place to place.

I want to plunge
Like a soldier into the bloody fight
To sleep beside campfires
In the dark of night.

When I hear the mill-wheel turning
Then I don't know what I want--
Above all I want to die
Then all would be still.

Moonlight

It was as if the heavens
Had kissed the silent earth,
So that it could now
Dream of shimmering blossoms.

The wind went through the fields
The meadows softly waved,
The forests were a-rustling
The night was so clear and starry.

And my soul spread
Out wide its wings and
Flew through the silent landscape
As if it were flying home.

THE PILGRIM

We are placed on the threshold,
We don't know from where?
The morning glows brightly,
We feel a great urge to go out.
The sound and images of the earth,
Deep blue pleasure of spring,
Enticing us wildly and more wildly,
These are what stir our hearts.
Soon it becomes so sultry all around,
The world is hardly breathing,
Mountains, the castle and cool forests
Stand soundlessly, as if in a dream.
And a secret dread
Creeps into our minds
We long to go home
And we don't know which way to go.

FALL

Now fall is here,
It has taken its beautiful
Summer clothes from the fields
And strewn leaves,
While the winter wind
Covers the ground
Warm and gently with colorful foliage
Which, tired, has gone off to sleep.

Through the fields one sees travelling
A wonderfully lovely woman
And golden strands from her long hair
Touch the meadows and
She weaves and sings as she goes
Aya, my little flower,
Don't always look to others,
Aya, go off, go off to sleep.

And the birds in the air
Over blue mountains and lakes
Turn from afar to the cliff-tops
Where tall cedars stand,
Where with their golden swinging
Above the blessed tombs
Angels sing Hosannahs
At night in the silent breeze.

SONG

Freshly blow bright currents below.
Outside colorful ships bow in silence,
While currents and ships and the colors
Are all asking: why cry?
I feel so glad, I feel so sad
When I see spring a-travelling.

For many springs I have sat above,
A rainbow standing high in the sky
And over the valleys, meadows, and waves
Silence, like a distant song, is heard
Sailing ever farther with its heavenly image--
For currents and ships are never still.

ON MY CHILD'S DEATH

The hours ring out from afar,
It is already deep night,
The light burns so gloomily
Your little bed is made.

Only the winds wander
Moaning through the house,
We sit alone inside
And listen to the night.

It is as if you must softly
Come knocking at the door.
You were only lost,
And now come tired back home.

We poor, poor fools!
We are the ones out wandering
Lost in the darkness--
You found your way home long ago.

GOOD NIGHT

Peaks and forests already stand
Bathed in evening gold,
A little bird asks among the branches
Should it greet my true love?

O little bird, you have spoken falsely,
She no longer lives in the valley,
Fly up to heaven's rainbow,
And greet her there one last time for me!

FAITHFUL

Like a wanderer in a dream,
Who still cries out in his sleep,
As his homeland appears
Between the golden banks of cloud:

So when the spring blossoms
Over mountains and deep valleys,
I often see your errant image
As if I had cried out from inside;

And so with wonderful emotions
Like in dreams, half known,
Eternal song sources wander
Through my heart confusing me.

HARMONY

1.

Oh beloved, wonderful, beautiful life,
Will you lead me once again?
Should I say good-bye once more
And flee my peaceful studies?

The doors and windows are open,
Outside the messengers of spring appear
Chirping larks arise,
While echoes settle peacefully in the woods.

Fine, it does not help to fight it,
Now deep in my heart I must say:
O beloved, wonderful, beautiful life,
Where will you lead me to this time!

2.

High above the silent heights
There stands a house in the woods,
It seemed so lonely
When seen through the forest.

A girl sits inside it
At her silent evening's chores
Spinning silk threads
For her wedding dress.

THE NIGHTINGALE

On lovely days in spring
When the blue breeze sighs,
I wish I could fly with the birds
And enjoy the newness of love.
There is a chattering in the sky;
And lightning plays
In the distance through the trees
All night long with wonder
It keeps the nightingales awake
With its errant flashes,
And all over the holy ground
They make known in the loneliness,
What they all, all of them recognize:
Rustling in the trees
Like humans in dark dreams.

In The Forest

A wedding party passes along the mountainside
I heard the singing birds flutter
Many a horseman shone and horns blared,
It was a happy piece of hunting!

And before I knew it, the sounds died away,
The falling night covered the globe,
Only the trees whispered from the mountains
While I trembled in the depths of my heart.

TWILIGHT

Dusk will spread the birds' wings,
Strangely rustling in the trees,
Clouds appear like heavy dreams--
What does all this dread mean?

Do you have a deer, dearer than all others?
Don't let it graze alone,
Hunters go through the woods blaring
Calling out and wandering on.

Do you have a friend down here?
Don't trust him at this time,
Friend, it's true--with eye and voice,
Yet plotting war while feigning peace.

Things that lie down tired today;
The morning will raise up newborn.
Much remains lost in the night--
Take care, be watchful and alert!

AT NIGHT

I wander through the silent night,
While the moon crawls silently, secretly
Out of the dark cloud-depths,
Here and there in the valley
The nightingale awakes,
Then all is still and silent once more.

O wonderful night-time song:
From afar the land of rivers flows,
Light shimmers through the darkening trees--
My thoughts become confused,
My singing is errant here
Like a shout from out of dreams.

THE WANDERING MUSICIAN

1.

I love a life of wandering,
Alighting wherever I can,
If I were prone to worry,
Why it just wouldn't suit me.

In the cold, without shoes
I know lovely old-time songs
Among their melodies I travel,
Not knowing where to sleep to night.

Beautiful women cast their eyes on me,
Which means: I am pleasing to them,
If I could only amount to something
I am a sorry soul, aren't I?

God may want to give you a servant
And a house with courtyard too!
But if we two stood together,
My singing might forsake me.

2.

If the weather were warm and sunny,
Mild and blue as it is in foreign countries,
I would walk with my mandolin
Through the glistening meadow.

In the night my sweetheart would listen
At the window sweetly sleepless,
She would secretly wish me and herself
--both of us a beautiful night.

If the weather were warm and sunny,
Mild and blue as it is in foreign countries,
I would walk with my mandolin
Through the glistening meadow.

3.

I travel over a green land,
When winter is finally through,
My lute hangs from a golden band
Which I wear around my neck.

The morning casts a reddish glow,
Which my heart discovers,
Then I grip the strings tightly,
And hear God's love resounding.

The stream flows on its silver way,
From afar bells are ringing,
My soul calls out: be well!
And people's greetings echo my joy.

My heart is made of diamond,
A bloom of precious stone,
Which shines over the dark land
In a thousand lovely sheens.

From a castle into the distance
A young woman looks down,
Her beloved holds her in his arms,
And they look down at me.

How beautiful you are! While out in the forest
Waters tumble plashing down,
In the green trees commanding
My heart to remain alert and free!

The sun leaves us in darkness,
To wash itself in the sea,
Then I rest from the day's feast
Devoutly in the rose-colored cool.

High above in silent night
The moon leads the golden sheep,
God watches over the round earth,
While I sleep down here below.

How far away is all false splendor!
Sleep well on the silent earth,
God protect your heart in heaven,
So that you know no sorrow!

4.

If you are sometimes in a bad humor,
I press you tenderly to my heart,
So that it almost takes my breath away.
I carress you in sweet playfulness
Like someone truly mad for love.
Gently I lean my cheek against you
And you sing delicately in my ear.
It is true that the sound makes the cat meow
and the dog bark and howl in the yard,
And the neighbor makes a terrible face and swears.
But why should we care about the reaction of the world,
Sweet, beloved violin!

5.

Discontently they loll and mope
On the broad benches without a sound
The lazy ones yawn and stretch themselves
While the bold ones look for fights.

Then from afar I come a-wandering,
Through the town in the cool twilight,
I stand in the middle of the circle
I greet people and take out my fiddle.

And as I brandish the bow,
Sounds fill the circle
And they move their bodies

From the depths of their hearts.

And now begins the clinking of glasses
And a waltz one, two, three,
The more I play the more they move
No one stops to ask why?--

Now each will give the fiddler
A little something with their hands
Then I go beyond fiddling
And become a real musician.

And they see him mount happily
Up into the forest heights,
They hear him playing from afar,
And contented they all go home.

Yet in the passages of the forest
I rest for many an hour,
Only distant nightingales
Sound out in the depths of the evening.

And the night rustles so softly
Through the forest loneliness,
While I dream up new ways
Of refreshing the human heart.

6.

Through fields and beech halls
Sometimes singing, sometimes happily quiet,
Above all be quite friendly
You who choose to travel!

When in the east it begins to glow,
The world still wide and silent:
Then right through my heart floats
The beautiful blossomtime!

The lark as morning messenger
Flits through the air,
With a fresh travelling note

That rings out through forest and heart.

O joy, to look down from the mountain
Far over forest and stream,
And high above the blue,
Clear dome of heaven!

From mountains little birds come flying
And clouds dart by so swift
Thoughts are flying over
Both birds and wind.

The clouds fly down below,
Little birds flit downwards too,
While thoughts and songs
Rise into the realm of the sky.

THE GYPSY WOMAN

At the crossroads, I listen, when stars gleam
And fires glow in the forest,
And where the first dog howls from afar,
Then my love will soon be appearing.

And as the day comes in gray, through the woods
I see a cat creeping along,
I shoot at her nut brown fur
As though she would leap away!--

"It's too bad that you bother me just for a fur!
My treasure must look like anyone else's:
Brown and short hair of Hungarian cut
And a heart happy to wander."

THE WANDERING STUDENT

In the most pleasant weather
All the little birds sing
But if the rain rustles on the leaves,
Then I sing for myself alone.

Even if the lightning flashes brightly,
Then my eyes will not find
Anything to trouble
My peaceful disposition.

Free from Mammon I will walk
Through the fields of science,
Thinking seriously and sometimes taking
A welcome taste of wine.

When I am tired of studying,
When the moon strolls softly by,
Then I turn to music making
Before a beautiful woman's window.

THE PAINTER

From the clouds, when in an evening landscape
The creatures awake,
God's hand stretches
And draws through the silent meadow
Powerfully the shapes contours
Of stream, forest and precipice.

Wake up! Wake up! the larks cry out,
Aurora plunges its rays
Dreamily into the fragrant air
Beginning in mountains and valleys
'Round about a heavenly painting
Of sea, and land, and air.

And through the light-kissed silence
Out of wondrous curls
An angel glances.--
Then the frightened forest rustles,
The morning bells ring,
And the peaks stand amazed.

O light eyes, earnest and mild,
I cannot leave you alone!
Soon once more wild
Cares and hate will rage here
Through the confusing streets
Lead me on, o godlike image!

THE SOLDIER

1.

Even if my horse isn't pretty
Still, he is quite clever,
He takes me to the castle in the dark
He is fast enough for me.

Even more the castle is splendid
With its walls and gardens
Every night a girl walks
Here and is quite friendly.

And even if the little one isn't
The most beautiful in the world,
There is no one else,
Who pleases me so much.

And if she talks of wooing:
Then I climb on my horse--
I will remain at liberty,
And she in the castle.

2.

You must risk it, quickly take treasures
For I hear steps behind us in the night,
Climb up on my horse quickly
And kiss me now, lovely, wild child,
Quickly,
Death is a sudden companion.

SEAMAN'S FAREWELL

Ade, my treasure, you don't love me,
I am too poor for you.
For you have wandered by moonlight
And heard the sweet ringing,
Of a mermaid singing; the night is gentle,
The silent clouds wander
Then think of me, it is my wife,
Yet now you seek another!

Ade, your landowner, the Musketeer!
We will ride on wild horses,
Prancing and kicking sharply
Before many cliff-castles,
The waterspirits are as fast as lightning
Plunging into the deep night,
The shark bites, the seagulls cry--
It is a merry fight!

Stretch out on your bearskin
With your lazy limbs at home,
God the father looks out the window,
And sends the Flood once again,
Fieldweavers, Knights, Musketeers,
They all must drown
While on a refreshing wind we
Race off into paradise.

THE PLAYERS

Early mornings through the mountain gap
We announce Victoria!
A lark travels through the air:
"The Players are already here!"
A tower stretches out
Sleepily through the morning gray,
As if out of a dream it traces
The stream through the silent meadow,
Where your eyes suddenly
Glance at the brook,
At the forest, at the green forests
And you hear their happy call!

It's a joyful trip
The oaks, fresh and cool,
Make shadows where we eat,
And lay a green table for us.
For breakfast there is music
From the happy, little birds.
The forest, when they pause,
Joins in quite wonderfully
Making the tree-tops rustle
As if to bless our meal,
And show usn through the branches
The wide valley far below.

Far below there is a garden,
Where a beautiful lady lives,
We cannot wait too long,
We gaze through a barred gate,
To where the white statues stand,

There it's still and cool,
The water fountains plash,
The lilacs' scent is heavy.
We wander along singing
In the early morning time,
She hears our chiming in a dream,
But we have already moved on.

Before The City

Two musicians arrive here
From the forest and from off in the distance,
The one is head over heels in love,
The other would like to be.

They stand here in the cold wind
And sing beautifully and fiddle:
Won't a sweet, ethereal girl
Show herself at the window?

WOOD SPIRIT WITH ACTORS

I am wearing out my travelling shoes
Since I am always on my feet--
What will we do now
Before so many clever people?

We raise the roofs from off of the houses
And rustle the curtains
And stretch them to the heavens
So they sound like streams and forests!

And out of the clouds that are so soft
They all stand next to each other,
And tuck things away in confusion,
People, princes, and wood spirits.

Some trudge tiredly on,
The others linger a while
It's the old play that we do so well
And never bring to an end.

And no one knows the last act
In the play, not even the players.
Only he above who keeps the beat
Knows how things will end.

The Traveller in Love

1.

Then I will go out in a wagon,
You are so far away from me,
And wherever it takes me,
I will always be beside you.

Forests and cliffs fly past
And beautiful, deep valleys,
And larks high in the air,
As if your voice were calling.

The sun shines happily
Over the entire preserve,
I have wept for joy
And silently sing to myself.

From mountains I descend,
The posthorn sounds out over the land,
Yet, my soul is merry within me;
I greet you from the bottom of my heart.

2.

I go through darkened streets
And wander from house to house,
I cannot seem to settle down,
Everything seems so sad.

Many men and women come and go,
They all seem so happy,
They travel and smile and build,
So that my senses take leave of me.

Often when I see bluish strands
Fly by over the rooftops,
At the sunshine wandering above,
Clouds gathering in the heavens:

Tears accompany me
Welling from my eyes
For all those who love wholeheartedly
All seem so far from here.

3.

Song, with tears half written,
From here over mountains and cliffs,
Where my beloved awaits,
Fly through the blue air!

If she is pink and happy, say:
I am sick to the bottom of my heart;
If she cries at night and thinks quietly all day,
Yes, then say: I am healthy!

If your true love has left you,
Now, so ends all joy and need,
And to all who love me,
Fly away and say: I am dead!

4.

Ah my love I leave you behind,
My lovely, hearty child,
Now many men will be watching
They have bad ideas for you.

They would love to disturb
The happy party here on earth,
Ah, if love should end,
Then they would take the rest.

And all the green places,
Where we went in the woods,

Have now become something else,
They are now so silent and cold.

Now in the cold heavens
Many a thousand stars are placed,
Shining their golden swarm
High over the snow-covered field.

My soul is so uneasy,
The streets are empty and dead,
Then I take up my lute,
And sing out of a need for music.

Ah, if I were in a quiet heaven!
Cold winds blowing against windows,
Sleep easy, my beloved, sleep,
True love will always endure.

5.

Green were the pastures
The skies blue,
We sat together
In the glistening meadow.

Were there nightingales
That still sang;
Larks, which sang out
In the warm air?

I hear the songs,
In the distance, without you,
The spring will return,
But not for me.

6.

Clouds wandering towards the forest,
Clouds flying over the house,
If only I could fasten myself to you
And fly with you so far away!

All day long I rove along through the forest
Filled with thoughts I sit quite still,
I grip the strings lightly,
Then once again all is silent.

Beautiful, peaceful faces
Occur, where I am standing,
Happily I must write, and create,
At the same time there is pain.
Many songs that I have written
Over the many long years,
When the world with true love
Has cast its loving glance;

If I find myself worried again:
I become wonderfully calmed,
For it was o so long ago,
That I was led to song.

The clouds drive on,
All the birds are awake,
And the region glistens warmly,
Widely and happily decorated.

Rain flies away with speed,
The sun shines between the clouds
And your house and your garden stand
In the forest in silent light.

Then you will know no more pain,
Though your beloved must--
And the magic spell of pain
Still consumes my heart.

RETURN TRIP

With my fiddle-playing,
That has rung out so beautifully,
Now I pass through many places
On my way back to the city.

I roam through the streets,
So dark in the night,
Everything is so desolate
I had imagined it otherwise.

At the well I stand for a long time,
It rustles on as before,
Many a one passes by,
But they do not know me anymore.

Then I hear fiddle-playing, pipes,
The windows glow from afar,
Many strangers, joyful people
Turn and twirl in dance.

And my heart and mind were burning
Driven out into the wide, wide world,
Where the musicians were playing,
I fell down in the field.

IN A CASTLE

Sleeping through the watch
Up above stands the knight,
Over us all go rain showers,
And the forest rustles against the fence.

Overgrown beards and hair,
And stony breast and curls
He sits many hundreds of years
Above in the silent cloister.

Outside all is silent and peaceful,
Everyone lives down in the valley,
Forest birds sing alone
On the empty window sills.

A wedding party winds along below
On the Rhein in the sunshine
Musicians play softly
And the beautiful bride is weeping.

Annual Fair

Are these the houses, are these the streets?
Ah, I do not know where I am!
I left a girl here long ago,
And many years have passed since then.

Out the windows beautiful women
Cast me loving looks,
But none can look as fresh,
As my true love's face.

At the house I knock anxiously--
Still the windows remain empty,
She is long since gone,
And no one knows me anymore.

And all around the sellers call out,
Sweet wares, colorful things,
Men and women go for strolls
Through the colorful rows of stalls.

Graceful leaps, friendly glances,
Many fleeting love-words,
Handshakes, secret signals
The flow of things takes them all in.

And my beloved I even saw
Sadly in the happy throng,
And a handsome man next to her
Leading her proudly on his earnest arm.

All puffed out were mouth and cheeks,
And her gaze was broken,
Strangely she looked silent and long,

Even after I had passed.--

And so ends the day of play
Through the streets the wind goes whistling--
No one knows how our hearts
Are deeply torn by sorrow.

Away from Home

I hear the brooks rustle
In the forest to and fro
In the forest in the rustling
I do not know where I am.

The nightingales cry
Here in the loneliness,
As if they wanted to tell
About the good old days.

The moonbeams flit,
As if I saw below me
A castle lying in the valley
That is so far from here!

As if it were in the garden
Filled with roses white and red,
My beloved waits for me;
Though she is long since dead.

LONGING

The stars sparkle so brightly,
I stand alone at the window
Listening to the distant sounds
Of a posthorn in the silent landscape.
My whole heart leaps to life,
Then I secretly say to myself:
Ah, if I could only travel with them
In the splendid summer night!

Two young friends climb
Up above along the cliff.
I listen to them singing their way
Along the silent path:
About dizzying cliff-faces
Where the trees listen so softly,
About springs which from the cliffs
Plunge into the forest night!

They sang of marble statues,
Of gardens over whose stones
The foliage grows wild in the darkness,
Of palaces in the moonshine
Where the maidens listen by windows
When lute's song stirs their breasts,
And the sleepy springs go plashing
In the splendid summer night.

FAREWELL

O broad valleys, o heights,
O beautiful, green forests,
You contain all my desire and despair
The site of my devotion.
Since outside, always deceived,
Bustles the busy world,
Strike the bow once more
With your green tent all around!

When the day begins
The mists rise glistening from the earth,
The birds call happily,
So that they resound in your heart:
Then in sighs there passes away
The sad earth's song,
Then shall you rise up again
In youthful splendor!

In the forest there is written,
A silent, earnest saying
To live and act rightly,
Which is the treasure of mankind.
I have read it through
The saying, simple and true,
And through my whole being
It is ineffably clear.

Soon will I leave you,
And become a stranger in a strange land
Wander down colorful streets
Watching life's passing play;
And amid all of this life

Your earnest strength will remain
To raise me from my loneliness.
So that my heart never grows old.

WHEN THE ROOSTER CRIES

When the rooster cries from the roof,
The moon extinguishes its lamp,
And the stars return from their watch
May God protect our lands and house!

THE MORNING

The first morning ray filters
Through the silent, mist-filled valley,
The awaking forest and the hill rustles
With those who can take to flight!

And his little hat is cast into the air
By the man who happily calls out:
As the songs also lift me up
So will I sing out joyfully!

Outside, o man, in the wide world,
When the heart is troubled with sorrow;
Nothing is so dark in the night,
But that the morning light sets things right.

PEACE AT NOON

Over mountains, rivers and valleys,
Silent desire and deep torments
Interweave, shimmer, glisten!
Thinking over the day's warmth
In the dark blue sultry day,
And the eternal feeling
That was unknown to you,
Meets secretly, heavy and slow
Out of the whirling of festive feet,
Out of the innocent breast,
In a silent but widening circle.

THE EVENING

All loud desires now silent fall:
The earth rustles as if in dream
Wonderfully through all the trees,
Yet the heart hardly comprehends;
Old days, soft sorrows,
And gentle passing glances
Dart like lightning through my mind.

THE NIGHT

How beautiful it is here to dream away
The night in silent glade
While in dark trees
Old fairytales ring true.

Mountains in the moonlight
Stand as if in thought,
And through their overgrown ruins
The springs go their way lamenting.

Then tiredly on her mat
Beauty is now at rest,
Night covers with cool shadows
My beloved lady.

There is a fleeting complaint
In the silent forest splendor,
The nightingale calls out
Above her all night long.

The stars go round and round--
When will you come, o morning wind?
And lift all of the shadows away
From the dreaming child?

Already there is rustling in the trees,
The larks soon awake--
So I will truly dream away
The night in the silent woods.

Way Pointer

"Now you must strike out to the right,
Creep along and listen close,
Then take off quickly on the run--
So that you can get away."

"Thanks! but amid the world's confusion
Tell me, o wise master,
Which is the way to Heaven?
That is what I want to know."

DECEPTION

I rested after wandering
The moon had just risen,
Then I peered far across the land
At the old Tiber running by,
In the forests there were ruins,
Palaces on silent peaks
And gardens in the moonlight--
O foreign land, how beautiful you are;

And when the night came to an end,
The earth shone so wide,
I saw a shepherd seemingly suspended
Above a cliff in the loneliness.
Then I wondered all confused:
Will I reach Rome today?
He bent down and turned half around:
You are not very smart!
A festive laugh fell from his lips
I could see that he was drunk,
But then it passed from my mind--
In fact it was all just a dream.

BEAUTIFUL COUNTRY

The tree-tops rustle and shake
As though at this time the old gods
Were making the rounds
Of the half-sunken walls.

Here behind the myrtle trees
In dark and secret splendor,
What will you tell me in my confused dreams
O fantastic night?

All the stars are sparkling over me
And with a glowing look of love,
Drunkenly the distance speaks
Of a future happiness!--

LOVE ABROAD

1.

Everyone says their love is happy,
Only I remain alone,
So some will surely ask:
Who does the stranger belong to?
And so I must go, like a wave in a stream,
An unheard ripple on the threshold of spring.

2.

How coolly I roam at night,
My trusty guitar in hand!
From the heights I send greeting all around
To the heavens and the silent land.

How everything has changed,
Where I was so happy in the valley.
How still the forest! only the moon wanders
Above the high hall of beeches.

The festive voices have died away
And all the color of life's course,
Only the river, cast into the valley,
Sometimes flickers with silver.

And nightingales as if in dreams
Often awake one with their sweet call,
They rustle in the trees with memories
Secretly whispering everywhere.

Joy does not fade away
And the day's glow and happiness

They still sing secretly to me
Remaining in my deepest heart.

And happily I grip the strings,
O girl, on the other side of the stream,
You listen carefully and hear from afar
And know the singer by his greeting!

3.

Over the glistening peaks
From afar it comes like a greeting,
Whispering, bending the treetops
As if they wanted to kiss.

Is it then so beautiful and mild!
Voices travel through then night,
Singing secretly of the scene--
Ah, I have woken to joy!

You springs, don't splash so loud!
For the morning mustn't know!
That in the gentle wells of the moon's night
I silently sank my luck and sorrow.--

4.

Now I really want to wander!
Even the girls
Listen at the window
The springs rustle from afar
Out of the shimmering bushes
They chatter so loudly, so lovely,
I recognize the sound;
I hear my love!

Watch out child! at night
Love comes a-wandering,
And calls softly to the others,
For footsteps will awaken
The gods in their halls

And send us outside,
Though the poet brings them all
Back to you in the house.

THE HAPPY MUSICIAN

The woods, the woods! God keeps them green,
Gives good shelter and takes nothing for it.

In the green forest we stop for rest
Pride is not our goal,
In the inn, where we did not pay,
There was far too much respect
The owner didn't want to let us go,
They left off drinking and playing cards,
The whole city was in the streets,
And from the benches with great joy
The students rushed out of school,
The crowds increased from house to house,
Waved their hats and revelled and teemed,
The watchmen, the wardens, the beadles
Walked about wooing like princes,
Wishing everyone, everyone the royal treatment.
We, however, crept through the market square
Between the people with our wander-staff,
Holding aloft the tambourine which resounded.

To the woods, to the woods, to the lovely, green woods!

And then everyone went to bed,
The woods ignites will-o-wisps,
Frogs bring a serenade,
Bats whir silently by,
And in the river upon wet stones
The old merman yawns loudly,
Stroking his beard in the moonshine,
Asking a will-o-wisp who we are?
But suddenly he disappeared,

While high above blew the wind
Through the tree tops went the wild huntsman,
Swirling over the old towers
And the weather-cock crowed to us below:
Would you like to try sitting under its roof?
O Cock Robin, your house is in ruins,
An owl sits on the window,
And the forest rustles from all the gates.

The woods, the woods, the beautiful, green woods!

And once when tired we see the sparkling
Of a golden city, silent across the land,
At Saint Peter's Gate they are beckoning:
"Just come in here, Mister Musician!"
The angels make requests from the battlements
For they are the first to recognize us,
As the silver kettledrums are hit,
Saint Peter himself strikes the cymbals,
And many fiddles hang
From heaven, Celicia begins to play,
Through it all: Let him live long! they exclaim and shout,
Others sling from the wall into the air
Stars, comets,
Such splendid fireworks,
Singeing Saint Peter's Beard, so that he laughs,
And we return home, dear woods, good night!

WANDERSPEECHES

1.

It turns out quite differently than you thought:
While you appear pink and happy,
The spring and the sunshine are gone,
The precious present has turned quite black;
And hardly have you cried yourself out;
Everything laughs again, the sun shines once more--
It is quite different than what others thought.

2.

Heart, in your sunlit days
Do not hold anything grudgingly back!
Always happy friends
Are met by the happy person.

The stars go down: wandering alone
You may go to the end of the world--
Don't count on anyone
Other than God who is ever faithful.

3.

Why will you make this stop
And remain in this part of the world?
Soon the coach will blow its horn
And you will leave everything behind.

4.

The lark greets morning's first ray,
That enkindles in its breast

While only the lazy night, through with it all,
Creeps across the forest floor.

And you desire, o child of man, a chance
To yield to despair?
What is your little earth's trouble?
You must transcend it!

5.

The storm goes raging around the house,
I am no fool and yet I go out,
But when I am outside
I want to wrestle with it bravely.

6.

Eternal play of the waves!
You have already told many lies,
Many will never come back again.
And then the breakers awake
Again and again fresh risks,
False and happy like luck.

7.

The wanderer, far from home,
When the earth all around falls silent,
The sailor on the sea's loneliness,
When the stars rise out from the flood:

They both look and read
In the silent night
What they did not know or suspect:
When it was still a happy day.

The Wandering Poet

I do not know what it will say!
I have hardly stepped over the threshold,
Just as a lark whirls around
Joyfully through the blue sky.

There is grass all around, the flowers
Set like jewels or pearls in hair,
The slender poplars, bushes, and seeds
Bow in greater state.

The brook flows along as asked,
And where the wind parts the tree-tops
Cast stolen glances on me
As if she were my dear bride.

Yes, I come tired to rest at night,
The nightingale before the door
Brings me news, as soon glow-worms
Will light up in the forest.

In vain! It happens at once,
No poet travels unknown,
The happy springtime notices me,
Like a king entering his realm.

MEMORY

1.

Gentle rustling in the tree-tops,
Birds arriving from afar,
Springs spurting from the peaks,
Tell me where my homeland lies.

Today in a dream I saw it again
And from all the mountains came
Such a greeting to me below
That I began to cry.

Ah, here on foreign heights:
Men, springs, mountains, and trees,
The whirring of the tree-tops
Everything is like a dream.

2.

The distant homeland peaks
The high and silent house,
The mountains from which I look
Each spring down into the countryside,
Mothers, friends, and brothers,
I have often thought of them,
They all greet me again
In the silent moonlight.

HOMESICKNESS

Whoever would wander abroad
Must go with their beloved,
The others rejoice and leave,
The stranger remains alone.

What do we know, dark tree-tops,
Of the good old days?
Ah, the land behind the peaks,
How far it is from here!

Best of all I watch the stars,
Which shine as if I went to them,
I love to hear the nightingale
She sang before my gate.

The morning is my joy!
I rouse myself in silence;
To the highest mountains far away:
Greetings, Germany, from the bottom of my heart!

On The Border

The faithful mountains stand watch:
"Who's playing in the silent morning
Who do I hear from across the heath?"
But I saw the mountains
And laughed to myself with great joy,
And called out from a happy breast
Words and forest cries like:
Long live Austria!

Only when I recognize the region
The birds and brooks greet me so fine
And the woods in the surrounding landscape,
The Danube glints far below,
Saint Stephen's Tower, in the distance,
Peaks over the mountains and would see me with pleasure,
And if it is not so, then it will soon be,
Long live Austria!

WANDERING SONG OF THE PRAGUE STUDENTS

To the South now will fly
The birds all at once,
Many wanderers happily toss
Their hats in the morning sun.
They are the master students
Who go out through the gate,
On their instruments
They blow their fond farewells:
Into the far and wide
Goodbye o Prague, we go into the wide open!
And let him have peace
Who sits beside the fire!

At night we wander through the towns,
The windows glimmer from afar,
Many beautifully attired people
Drag themselves to the windows.
We play in front of their doors
And are surely thirsty,
That comes from playing music,
Innkeeper, Sir, a fresh drink!
And guests for a pittance
With a bottle of wine
He who leaves his house--
Blessed is that man!

Now blows through the forest
The cold winter wind.
We strike out through the fields,

Wet with snow and rain,
Our coats flying in the wind,
Our shoes have holes,
Then we blow quickly
And sing out once more:
Blessed is the man
Who remains at home
And sits by the fire
And enjoys tranquility.

RETURN TRIP

Who is that out there?--Open up, quick!
Already the sparkling field is well mannered
It is the happy morning wind
That comes piping from out the forest.

A migratory bird, the clouds, and I,
We travel on a wager,
And we all think: hurry up,
We'll find them still asleep!

Now we are all outside,
Those indoors exchange kisses!
We crash suddenly through the door:
And bring noise, scents, and forest murmurs.

I come from far off Italy
And will tell you the news,
Of the mountain Vesuvius and Rome's star
The old tales of wonder.

There sings a fairy by the blue sea,
The drunken myrtles whisper--
But nothing pleases me as much,
As the German forest rustling!

THE MARRIAGE

What a chirping it is!
Through the blue the swallows tweet
And cry out: "They have kissed!"
From the trees the red throats watch.

The Storch shifts from leg to leg
"Now I must go fishing--"
The evening like in a dream
Looks on from silent peaks.

And as in a dream from the peaks
At night I creep around my beloved's house,
The clouds pass by
And extinguish the stars.

THE ERRANT MUSICIAN

From silent youth's innocent protection
A reckless mood has driven me out
And since then I have been outside and free
So that I can't find my way back home again.

Through life I hunt many deceitful images,
Who is that hunter? Who is the quarry?
The wind blows clipping through my hair,
Ah world, how cold and clear you are!

You pious child in the silent house,
Don't look so longingly out the window!
Don't ask me, child, where from and where to.
I don't even know myself where I am!

My heart is torn by sins and sorrows,
We rave in despairing desire,
I break off in flight flowers for a bouquet,
No happy wreath can be made from it!--

I want to plunge into the deepest forest,
To shout my pain out of my breast,
I would like to ride to the end of the world,
Where the moon and sun go down together.

Where dizziness begins in eternity,
Like a sea, so horribly still and wide,
There end all rivers and sails fall away,
There it may be peaceful in the end.

LAST HOMECOMING

The winter morning shines so clear,
A wanderer comes from far away,
He shakes off the frost, it spikes his hair,
The lovely distance has lied to him,
Now he wants to stay and rest,
He knocks on his father's door.

Those are dead who once lived here,
The house and home have changed,
Strange people gaze at him,
As if he had risen from the grave;
He looks deep within his heart,
And quickly he goes off to the meadows.

There, no birds sing clear and bright,
He leans against a tree,
The lovely garden is snowed under,
It is as if he were in a dream,
And as the morning bells ring,
He sinks down in the field.

And as he rises from prayer
Not knowing where to turn,
A lovely youth appears beside him,
And takes him gently by the hand:
"Come with me. Soon you will rest."--
He follows the sound, the voice is peace.

Now through the mountain loneliness
They seem to climb to heaven,
No bells ring at this height,
They look into the desolate silence

Of the land that withers behind them
Soon stars glow through the tree-tops.

The leader now takes up a torch
And raises it and silently steps,
By its light the silent night
Just like a cathedral extends above,
Where invisible hands build--
A secret fright takes hold of him.

He says: "what strange sound
Is brought by the wind
As if I heard distant streams,
And in-between bells are ringing?"
"That is the nightsong's breezes
Which praise God on the silent heights."

The wanderer says: "I can't go on--
Is it morning that is so blinding?
What sun lights up this land?"--
His friend turns the torch away from him:
"Now rest yourself one last time,
When you awake, we will be home."

FALL MAGIC
(A FOLKTALE)

I

Sir Ubaldo was out hunting on a pleasant fall evening when he strayed far from his men and went riding off into the forest mountains; there he saw a man in strange, colorful clothing rise up in front of him. The stranger did not notice him until he stood right before him. Ubaldo gazed with wonder, as this same man had a very neatly and splendidly stylish doublet that had, with the passage of time, become old-fashioned and incorrect. His face was handsome, but pale and wild, with an overgrown beard.

They both greeted each other, amazed, and Ubaldo told of how he had been unfortunate enough to have strayed there. The sun had already sunk behind the mountains, and this place was far from all human habitation. The unknown man asked the knight if he would spend the night with him, and he promised to show him at dawn the only path that would take him out of the forest. Ubaldo willingly agreed and followed his guide through the desolate forest ravine.

Soon they came to a towering cliff, at the base of which a spacious cave had been carved out. A large stone stood in the middle of the cave, and on the stone stood a wooden crucifix. A bed made of dried leaves formed the background of the hermitage. Ubaldo tied his horse at the entrance, while his host brought wine and bread, in silence. They sat down together, and the knight, for whom the clothes of the unknown man hardly appeared to indicate a hermit, could not keep himself from asking about his earlier life. "Don't ask who I am," answered the hermit forcefully, and then his face grew dark and unfriendly. In response, Ubaldo noticed, that this man listened attentively and then sank into a deep recollection, as he himself now began to remember the many travels and glorious

76

deeds he had experienced in his youth. Grown tired at last, Ubaldo stretched out on the proffered foliage and quickly fell asleep, while his host sat by the entrance to the cave.

In the middle of the night, the knight woke up from terrifying dreams. He sat up in semi-consciousness. Outside the cave, the moon shone very brightly on the silent ring of mountains. In the space before the cave, he saw his host wandering about, here and there, under the high, creaking trees. He was singing a song wholeheartedly, of which Ubaldo could approximately catch the following words:

Fears have driven me to this cliff,
Old tales follow me about--
Sweet sins, set me free!
Or throw me down
Hiding me in the bosom of the earth
Away from the magic of these songs.
And gathered into the earth's womb!

God! Ardently I would like to pray,
But the earth keeps its images
Always between you and me,
And all around the sighing forest
Fills my soul with horror
Strict God! I fear you.

Ah! Free me from my chains!
To set all men a-straight
You met a bitter death,
Wandering through the gates of hell,
Ah, how quickly I am lost!
Jesus, help me in my need!

The singer fell silent again, sat on his stone and appeared to mumble several incomprehensible prayers that seemed rather more like magic formulas. The rustling of the stream from the mountain and the light sighing of the pines strangely mingled with the prayers, and Ubaldo fell back, overcome by sleep, onto his bed.

Hardly had the first morning light shone through the tree-tops when the hermit stood before the knight to lead him out of the ravine. In a good mood, Ubaldo mounted his horse, and his strange guide walked silently beside him. They had reached the peak of the last mountain, when suddenly the valley they approached appeared filled with rivers, towns, and castles at their feet, in the most lovely morning glow. The hermit appeared surprised himself. "Ah, what a lovely world!" he said, obviously moved, covered his face with his hands, and hurried back into the forest. Shaking his head, Ubaldo took the well-known path back to his castle.

II

Curiosity soon drove Ubaldo back into the forest solitudes, and with some trouble he found the cave again, where the hermit, this time, was less dark and reserved.

Ubaldo had gleaned from the night-time songs that the hermit wanted to do penance for grave sins. But now it occurred to him that this intention strove unsuccessfully with the Enemy. In his conversation with the hermit, there was no sign of a soul that was truly at peace with God, and very often, as they sat talking with each other, a heavily repressed, earthly longing shot with an almost frightful power out of the flaming eyes of the man, so that his whole expression grew wild and seemed to transform him completely.

This moved the pious knight to make his visits more frequent in order to support the unstable man with the full force of an untroubled, innocent mind. As to his name and earlier position, the hermit kept silent, and this silence lasted a long time. It seemed that he shied away from his past. Still, with each visit, he appeared more at ease and trusting. Then, at last, the good knight succeeded in convincing him just that once to come back to his castle with him.

It had already become evening by the time they arrived at the castle. The knight made a warming fire in the hearth and brought out the best wine he had. The hermit already appeared to be comfortable on this, his first visit. He looked very carefully at a sword and other pieces of weaponry that hung on the wall and shone in the glow of the hearth, and silently observed the knight again. "You are lucky," he said; then, "And I notice your strong, joyful, manly form with true awe and respect, for you are not troubled by pain or joy. You move about and lead a peaceful life, which you take for granted like a sailor who knows clearly where he is to go and does not go astray at the wondrous song of the sirens. In your company, I often seem as a cowardly fool or a crazy man--there are those who are intoxicated by life--ah, how horrible it is to be sober again!"

The knight, who did not want to pass up this unusual emotion on the part of his guest, drew him out with good-willed intention, so as to, at last, learn his life's story. The hermit was thoughtful. "If you tell me," he said at last, "that you will always be silent about what I am going to say and allow me to leave out all names, then I will do it." The knight gave him his hand and said in a friendly tone what he wanted; he called his wife whose silence he guaranteed, so that she, too, could be bidden to take part in hearing this long desired tale.

She appeared, a child on her arm, the other led by the hand. She had a tall, lovely figure that was in the bloom of youth, silent and gentle like the setting sun, and whose declining beauty was reflected in her children. The stranger was quite stirred by the sight of her. He threw open the window and looked out for a while on the night landscape, so as to collect his thoughts. At peace again, he came back to them; they all moved closer to the fireside, and he began the following tale.

III

The fall sun remained lovingly warm over the colorful clouds, which decorated the valleys around my castle. The music fell silent, the party was over, and the happy guests went off in all directions. It had been a farewell party, which I had held for my youthful partner who, today, with his retinue, raises up the holy cross to help win the promised land for the Christian army. From our earliest youth, this pilgrimage of his was the only object of our common wishes, hopes, and plans, and I often feel an indescribable sadness at every silent, lovely morning moment when we stood under the high lindens on the rocky outcropping by the fortress and sat together dreaming of following the sailing clouds into some neighboring wonderland where Gottfried de Bouillon and the other heroes of shining honor lived and served. --But how everything inside of me has changed!

A girl, the flower of all beauty, whom I only saw once, and, though aside from that I knew nothing, right from the beginning, an unshakable love took hold of me and still holds me in the silent keep of these mountains to which I have been banished. Since I was not strong enough to fight it, I could not leave her, and so, I let my friend depart alone.

She was also at the party, and my head was swimming with more than enough happiness in reflections of her beauty. Only when she wanted to leave in the morning and I helped her onto her horse, I dared to reveal my thoughts to her, so that it was on account of her that I did not go on the pilgrimage. She said nothing about it, but looked at me with wide eyes and, as it appeared, terrified, rode quickly away.

With these words, the knight sighed, along with his wife who was certainly astonished. The stranger, however, did not notice it and kept right on speaking:

Everyone had gone away. The sun shone through the high bay windows into the empty chambers, where once only my lonely footsteps had wandered. I leaned for a long time out the alcove, while from the silent forest below, I heard the blow of a woodcutter. An undescribable longing emotion overpowered me in this loneliness of mine. I could not bear it any longer. I straddled my horse and road off hunting, to get some air for my stifling heart.

For a long time I road around here and found myself at last, to my amazement, on an almost unknown side of the mountains. I road on thoughtfully, my falcon on my wrist, through a wonderfully beautiful meadow, over which the setting sun sent slanting flashes of lightning. The fall cobwebs were blown about like veils through the clear blue air. High above the mountains, the parting songs of the migrating birds were heard.

Then I suddenly heard many hunting horns, which at some distance from the mountains appeared to answer one another. A few voices accompanied the songs. Never before had I heard music with such a wonderful longing as these tones, and even today I can recall many strophes of the songs, which wafted over me among the sounds:

Above bands, streaks of gold and red
The birds are flying away.
Thoughts are lacking comfort,
Ah! they do not find a port,
The dark laments of the horns
Strike your lonely heart.

Do you see the blue mountain's circle
Standing in the distance above the forest,
Streams in the silent landscape
Rustling far away?
Clouds, streams, cheerful birds,
They all fly down.

Golden are the locks of my hair,
Sweetly my young form is blooming--
Soon beauty is also paling,
Like the summer's glow,
Youth must bend its blooms,
All around the horns fall silent.

Slender arms to embrace,
Red mouth to kiss sweetly,
White breast, on which to rest,
Stretching, filled with love's greeting,
Calling you to the horns' resounding,
My sweet! Come, before they fade away!

I was confused by these sounds that pierced my entire heart. My falcon, once it heard the first horns resounding, was afraid, took off with wild cries, disappeared high into the air, and did not return. I, however, could not resist and followed the hunting horns' song farther on, my mind whirring now with the sounds coming from the distance, now coming back when the wind blew more closely.

So, at last, I came out of the forest and saw an empty castle, which lay on a mountaintop before me. Around the castle, from the peaks to the forest below, there smiled a wonderfully beautiful garden of the most striking colors, which seemed to cast a magic spell around the castle. All the trees and blossoming flowers, much more powerfully colored by the fall than usual, were purple, golden yellow, and the color of fire; high above asters, the last stars of the vanishing summer burned there in a manifold glow. The setting sun cast its sparkling rays right across this lovely height, on the fountains and the windows of the castle.

The blaring hunting horns, which I had heard from afar, had come from this garden; and in the middle of the glow and under the wild vineyard, I saw, terrified inside, the woman on whom all my thoughts centered, among the resounding horns, singing to herself, wandering around. She fell silent when she saw me, but the horns kept blaring away. Handsome servants in silk clothes rushed out to take my horse.

I raced through the finely gilded iron gate to the garden terrace where my beloved stood, and sank down at her feet, overcome by so much beauty. She wore a dark red garment with long veils, just like summer clothes in fall, with waving golden yellow locks held in place by a splendid aster fashioned out of a dark gemstone.

She raised me up lovingly and, with a peaceful and sorrow-broken voice, as if with love, said: "Handsome, unfortunate youth, how I love you! I have loved you for a long time, and when the fall begins its mysterious ceremony, my desire awakens with a new, irresistible power. Unfortunate man! How did you come into the compass of my horns? Leave me! Fly away!"

I shuddered at these words, and I asked her to tell me more and to enlighten me further. But she did not answer, and we walked silently beside one another through the garden.

It grew dark. Then an earnest nobility spread over her entire body.

"So you know," she said, "your young friend who left you today is a liar. I was compelled to become his beloved bride. Out of wild jealousy, he withheld his love from you. He isn't in Palestine, but is coming tomorrow to take me away to live in a well hidden castle protected from the eyes of all men. --Now I must part. We will never see each other again unless he dies."

With these words, she gave me a kiss on my lips and disappeared down the dark footpath. A stone from her aster glistened, gleaming coldly over her eyes as she went away; her kiss inflamed me with terrible lust that coursed through my veins.

Now I reflected upon her terrible words, which, in parting, she had cast like poison into my pure blood, and I wandered for a long time in the lonely paths around there, thinking about them. Tired, I cast myself at last on the stone steps before the castle gate; the hunting horns continued to resound, and I slumbered with odd thoughts of them.

When I opened my eyes, it was bright morning. All the doors and windows of the castle were closed fast; the garden and the whole region was silent. In this loneliness, I saw the image of my beloved and all the magic of yesterday evening with new morning-lovely colors in my heart, and I felt with my entire soul that I was loved again. Then, at times when I recalled her frightful words, I seized a thought: to rush away from here. But the kiss still burned on my lips, and I could do nothing else.

A warm and almost sultry wind came as if it wanted to bring back summer. I roamed dreamily in the nearby forest in order to distract myself with the hunt. Then I gazed at a tree-top and saw a bird with wonderfully beautiful feathers such as I had never seen before. When I pulled back my bow in order to shoot him, he quickly flew off to another tree. I followed him curiously, but the beautiful bird flew steadily on from tree-top to tree-top ahead of me, while his bright golden wingbeats glistened in the sunshine.

So, I came into a narrow valley that was ringed around by high cliffs. No raw winds penetrated this far; everything was green and blooming like in summer. A wonderfully lovely song seemed to be welling up from the middle of the valley. Astounded, I bent the branches of a thick bush next to which I stood, --and my eyes sank down drunk and blinded with the magic of this realm that appeared before me there.

A still fish pond lay in the circle of the high cliffs that extended their ivy and their sedge flowers. Many women bathed their beautiful limbs, while singing in the waters waving up and down. Above them all stood the woman, splendid and without covering and looking on, while the others sang and fell silent in the harmonious play, swishing their fingers in the waters as if charmed and bathing in the image of their own beauty, so that the drunken mirror of the water glistened. --Rooted, I stood for a long time enthralled. Then the lovely troop moved toward land, and I hurried away so as not to be discovered.

I plunged into the thickest forest to cool the flaming desire that was burning me up inside. But the farther I fled, the more lively the apparition of those youthful limbs appeared before my eyes.

Falling night met me in the forest. The entire sky had changed, and it had become dark; a wild storm raged over the mountains. "We will never see each other again, unless he dies!" I called out loudly within myself and ran as if I were being hunted by ghosts.

At times, it seemed that I had heard the horses hooves in the forest on either side of the passage, for I avoided human faces and ran from their noises whenever they seemed to come near. I often saw the castle of my beloved when I came to promontories. It stood in the distance; the hunting horns sang like last night. The glow of the candles shone like a mild moonlight through all the windows and lit up a magic circle of the nearby trees and flowers, while outside, the whole region was lost in storm and wild darkness.

No longer master of my thought, at last I climbed a high cliff at the bottom of which a forest stream poured out. When I came to the edge, I saw a dark shape seated on a stone, still and immobile as if it, too, were of stone. The clouds chased each other as if torn from the sky. The moon shone blood red in a glance before me--and I recognized my friend, the fiance of my beloved.

He stood up as soon as he saw me, sudden and tall so that I shivered inside, and he grabbed his sword. Angered, I fell upon him with both hands. Then, we wrestled for a while together until at last I cast him over the cliff wall and down into the bottom of the ravine.

Then, all was still in the depths of the forest and all around; only the stream below rustled more strongly, as if it were my former life buried under these whirling waves. All was gone forever.

Quickly, I rushed away from this dreadful place. Then, it seemed to me that I heard a loud, wild laugh ring out from the tree-tops below me. Then, in my craziness, I thought of the bird I had chased, and I seemed to see him again above me. --So, hunted, anxious, and half dazed, I ran through the wilderness and climbed over the garden walls to the woman's castle. With all my strength, I tore open the closed door. "Open up," I cried. "Open up; I have killed my blood brother! Now you are mine, on earth and in hell!"

Then the doorpanel was quickly opened, and the woman, more beautiful than I had ever seen her, came down inflaming kisses on my stormy ransacked breast.

Let me now fall silent about the splendor of the room, the scents of foreign flowers and trees, between which I saw beautiful women wander; of the waves of light and music; of the wild, nameless happiness I found in the girl's arms--

IV

Here, the stranger suddenly stopped. From outside, we heard a singular song flit past our ears through the window looking out on the town. It was just an isolated sentence, at times like a human voice, at other times ringing out like the highest tone of a clarinet, just as the wind when it blows over distant mountains, piercing one's heart and quickly moving on. --"Be at peace," said the knight. "We are used to it. There must be magic in the neighboring forest, and often in the fall, such sounds disturb the night around our castle. They go away as quickly as they come, and we think no more about them." --A great agitation appeared at work in the breast of the hermit, which he was only able to suppress with great effort. The sounds outside rang out again. The stranger sat like an unconscious ghost, lost in a deep thoughtfulness. After a long pause, he collected himself and went on, although no longer as peacefully as before. He continued his tale:

I noticed that the woman, at times, in the middle of her glances fell into an unintentional sadness when she looked out the window, as if the fall wanted to take its leave from all of the flowers. But a healthy, deep sleep through the night makes everything seem all right, and her wonderfully beautiful face, the garden, and the whole area around, glanced at me in the morning still with desire, fresh as newly born.

Only once when I was standing at the window with her was she silent and sadder than ever. Outside in the garden, the winter storms were playing with the fallen leaves. I noticed she often shuddered when she looked at the pale walls. All of her women had left us; the songs of the hunting horns now resounded only from afar, and then they, too, finally ceased. My beloved's eyes had lost all their glow and appeared to be closing. On the far side of the mountains, the sun went down and filled the gardens and the valleys around with a pale shimmer. Then, the girl entwined me with both arms and began to sing a strange song that I had never heard before and which, with a sorrowful harmony, carried throughout the house. I listened, surprised. It was as if I were given these tones with the evening red slowly sinking away; my eyelids could not stay open, and I fell into a dream-filled sleep.

When I awoke, it had become night, and all was silent in the castle. The moon shone very brightly. My beloved lay on her silken bed, sleeping stretched out beside me. I looked at her with wonder, for she was as white as a corpse, her curls hanging confused and as if tangled by the wind around her face and chest. All the rest lay there as before, as when I had fallen asleep, as it had been long ago. --I went to the open window. The area outside seemed changed and completely different than it had appeared before. The trees signed wonderfully. Then, I saw two men approach the area of the castle, talking darkly and gesticulating--always the same, bowing and swaying against one another here and there, as if they were trying to weave a cloth. I could not understand a thing, only that I often heard them name my name. --I glanced once more back at the girl's body that, even in the moonlight, seemed aglow. I felt as if I saw a stone statue--beautiful, but ice cold and unmoving. A gemstone flashed like a basilisk's eye on her chest; even her mouth seemed to be distorted.

A horror such as I had never felt in my life suddenly came over me. I left her lying there and wandered through the empty, desolate halls where there was no light. When I came out of the castle, I saw at some distance the two very strange men suddenly stop moving and stand still like statues. On the side under the mountain, I noticed a lonely group of maidens in snowwhite clothes, singing wonderfully and seeming to be busy breaking through the same webs and growing pale in the moonlight. This glance and this song added to my horror, and I leaped over the garden wall and fled. The clouds flew quickly across the sky; the trees rustled behind me. Breathlessly, I hurried on forward.

The night gradually became more silent and warmer. Nightingales called out in the bushes. Outside, deep under the mountain, I heard a voice; and old, long forgotten memories came back to me half darkly, back into my burned-out heart, as the most beautiful spring morning rose up over the mountains. --What is this? Where am I? I called out astonished, and I did not know the answer to the question of what had happened to me. Fall and winter had come and gone; it was again spring in the world. My God! Where had I been for so long?

I continued along the tops of the last mountains. Then, the sun came up splendidly. A delightful convulsion flew over the earth, streams, and castles in a flash. Humans, ah! Peaceful and happy they go round in their daily chores like always, while countless larks rejoice high up in the air. I got down on my knees and wept bitterly for my lost life.

I did not understand and still do not understand all that happened, but I did not want to get up in the hot, innocent world with my breast filled with sin and unbridled lust. Buried in the deepest solitude, I wanted to ask the heavens' forgiveness and not to see the human habitations anymore until I had, just once, washed away with hot, streaming tears, the faults I had in the past so clearly and surely known about.

For a year, I lived like this until you met me in that cave. Ardent prayers often rose from my angst-ridden breast, and I imagined at times, understandably, for I had found mercy before God; but it was only the soulful folly of occasional moments, and it was quickly gone. And now, the fall again spreads its wonderfully colorful net over mountains and valleys. Now, once again, there wafted the singular well-known tone of the forest. In my loneliness, dark voices reverberated in me and gave them answer. And, in the innermost horror, I still hear the bell-strokes of the distant cathedral, when they ring out Sunday morning over the mountains, reaching me as if they sought the old, silent realm of the God of childhood in my breast, though he is no longer there. --Look, it is a wonderful, dark realm of thought in the human breast. It shimmers crystal and ruby and all of these stone flowers of the depths. With frightened look back, magical sounds sign through them. You do not know where they come from and where they go. The beauty of earthly life shimmers upon us darkly, from above; the invisible springs rustle longingly, enticing, and they flow forever down--down!

V

"Poor Raymond!" called out the Knight, observing the stranger who was lost in the course of his tale, dreaming of long ago in the deep emotions of his soul.

"How in God's name do you know my name!" called out the stranger, as he leapt up like a lightning bolt from his seat.

"My God!" continued the knight and, with heartfelt love, embraced the trembling man in his arms. "Don't you recognize us? I am your old, true, blood-brother Ubaldo, and there is your Berta whom you secretly loved and whom you sent off on a horse after the farewell party at your castle. Certainly, time and an itinerant life erased our early, youthful pictures, and I could tell it was you from the moment you began your tale. I was never in a region such as you describe to me and never struggled with you on a cliff. I indeed went after that party to Palestine where I fought for many years, and the lovely Berta became my wife upon my return. Also, Berta has never seen you since the farewell party, and all that you have told us is pure fantasy. --An evil magic, each fall awakening anew and then again sinking down over you, my poor Raymond, has held you for several years tied up in its lying games. You have lived for months like a few days. When I came back to this land, no one knew what had become of you, and we believed you to have been long lost."

Out of joy, Ubaldo did not notice that his friend trembled even more deeply at each word. With wide and gaping eyes, he looked at the two of them and how they had changed. And now, for once, above their full and pleasant shapes, he recognized his friend and his youthful love, as the flames from the hearth played at casting shadows.

"Lost, everything lost!" he cried from the depths of his heart. He tore away from Ubaldo's arms and fled, arrow-quick, out of the castle and into the night and forest.

"Yes, lost. And my love and my whole life a long folly!" he said again to himself, and ran until all the lights of Ubaldo's castle had sunk away behind him. He unintentionally took the way back to his own mountain and arrived there as the sun rose.

It was once again a fall morning like it had been before when he had initially left the castle several years ago. And the memory of that time and the sorrow of the lost look, and the glory of his youth fell once more on his whole soul. The tall lindens by the stone courtyard rustled like before, but the clearing and the whole castle were empty and desolate, and the wind caressed everything through the broken bay windows.

He walked in the garden. It, too, was wasted and destroyed. Only a few late-blooming flowers gleamed here and there on the dry lawn. A bird sat on a tall flower and sang a wonderful song that filled his breast with unending longing. It was this same tone that he had heard yesterday evening during his tale in Ubaldo's castle, whispering to him. With sheer horror, he recognized now the beautiful golden yellow bird from the magic forest once again. -- But behind him, high on the bay window of the castle, he saw, during the song, a tall man over the wall--silent, pale, and sprinkled with blood. It was recognizably Ubaldo's likeness.

Disoriented, Raymond turned his face from the frightful silent image and looked at the bright day before him. Then, suddenly, the beautiful magic woman came up from below on a thin horse, laughing, in full bloom of youth, and passed by. Silver summer clothes flew behind her; the aster from her star cast long green and gold shimmerings over the heath.

Confused to distraction, Raymond rushed out of the garden toward the pure image.

The same song of the bird was taken up as it flew always before him. Generally, the farther it went, these strange tones turned into old hunting horn sounds that had once captivated him.

Golden my locks flutter
Sweetly my young body still blooms--

He listened now and again and in bits and pieces as it rang out again in the distance.

Brooks in the silent valley
Murmuring as they flow into the distance.

His castle, the mountain, and the whole world sank darkly behind him.

Give a full greeting
Offer yourself to the horns resounding.

Come, oh come! Before they fade away!

They faded once more--and in his lost delirium, the poor Raymond followed the sounds off into the forest and was never seen again.

CPSIA information can be obtained at www.ICGtesting.com
Printed in the USA
BVOW071032061211

277708BV00001B/37/P